Shellfish Aren't Fish

By Allan Fowler

Consultants

Linda Cornwell, Learning Resource Consultant,
Indiana Department of Education

Janann V. Jenner, Ph.D.

Sharyn Fenwick, Elementary Science/Math Specialist
Gustavus Adolphus College, St. Peter, Minnesota

Φ Children's Press ®
A Division of Grolier Publishing
New York   London   Hong Kong   Sydney
Danbury, Connecticut

Visit Children's Press® on the Internet at:
http://publishing.grolier.com

Designer: Herman Adler Design Group
Photo Researcher: Caroline Anderson

Library of Congress Cataloging-in-Publication Data

Fowler, Allan.
    Shellfish aren't fish / by Allan Fowler.
      p. cm. — (Rookie read-about science)
    Includes index.
    Summary: Provides information about oysters, clams, scallops, mussels,
and other sea animals that live in shells.
    ISBN 0-516-20802-0 (lib. bdg.)   0-516-26419-2 (pbk.)
    1. Mollusks—Juvenile literature. [1. Mollusks.] I. Title. II. Series.
QL405.2.F68   1998   97-26721
594—dc21   CIP
                                     AC

When is a fish not a fish?
When it's a shellfish.

We use the word "shellfish" to describe sea animals that have three things in common.

Lobster

Raw oysters

First, they have a shell.
Second, they are good to
eat. And third, they aren't
really fish.

American lobster

Coon stripe shrimp

Red crayfish

Deep swimming crab

There are many different types of shellfish.

Lobsters and shrimp,
crayfish and crabs are
all shellfish.

They belong to a group of
animals called crustaceans.

Crustaceans are like
insects because their bodies
are covered by a hard
substance instead of skin.

This book is about shellfish that belong to a group of animals called mollusks. A mollusk lives inside a hard shell, but its body is soft.

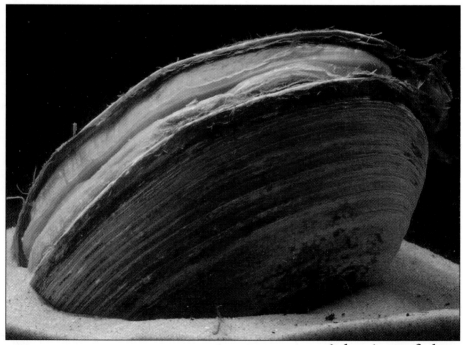

Atlantic surf clam

Conch snail

Every mollusk makes it own
shell. So in a way, a mollusk's
home—its shell—is a part of
the animal.

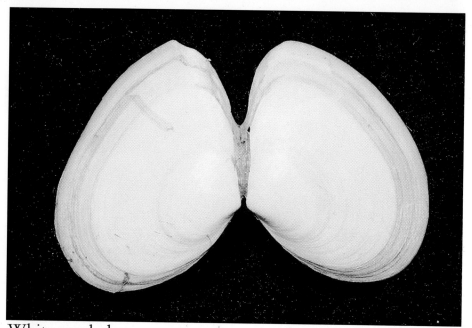

White sand clam

Clams, mussels, oysters, and scallops are all mollusks. They are called bivalves, which means that their shells have two halves.

The shell of a bivalve has
a hinge, just like the hinge
on a door.

Quohogue clam

The shell of a bivalve
is usually open.

Pacific pink scallop

When the animal senses danger, it uses the hinge to snap its shell shut.

Bivalves have something
else in common. Each
one has one strong foot.

A bivalve can use its
foot to move from place
to place.

The animal wedges its foot
between two rocks and
then drags its body and
shell along the seafloor.

A bivalve can also use
its foot to burrow in the
mud or sand.

A scallop has a shell
shaped like a fan. It is the
only bivalve that can jump
by spouting water out of
its shell.

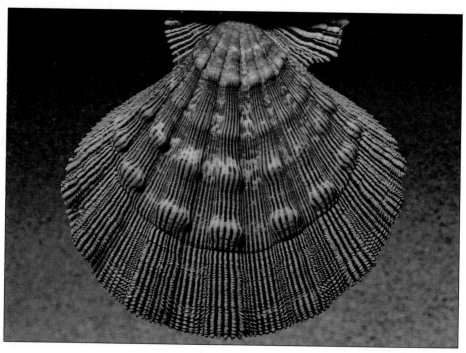

LEGAL LIMIT

Even though bivalves bury
themselves, people often
dig them up for food.

Oyster beds

Mussels and oysters
often live in large
clumps called "beds."

Oysters are usually eaten raw. Clams can be eaten raw or steamed. Mussels and scallops can be cooked many different ways.

Scallops

Most bivalves are small
enough to hold in your hand.

But some weigh as much
as 500 pounds! These giant
clams live along coral reefs
in the Pacific Ocean.

Sometimes a grain of sand gets inside a bivalve's shell. When it rubs against the animal's soft body, the bivalve coats it with a smooth material called mother-of-pearl.

Have you ever seen someone wearing a pearl necklace? There's a tiny grain of sand inside each white bead. The pearls used in jewelry come from oysters.

Queen conch

Not all mollusks have hinged shells. Conches (say "conks") live inside one-piece shells.

The shell of this sea snail has a graceful, spiral shape.

Top snail

Mother-of-pearl isn't just
found in pearls created
by bivalves.

If you look closely at the
inside of many shells, you
will see that they are lined
with mother-of-pearl.

Mother-of-pearl sparkles
with pretty colors, like those
you see on a soap bubble.

Some people like shells so
much that they collect them.

The next time you visit
the seashore, why not see
how many different kinds
of shells you can find?

Then, go to the library
and get a book that tells
you what kind of shellfish
made its home in each shell.

But don't look under "fish,"
because shellfish aren't fish.

Words You Know

crustacean

mollusk

conch

scallop

30

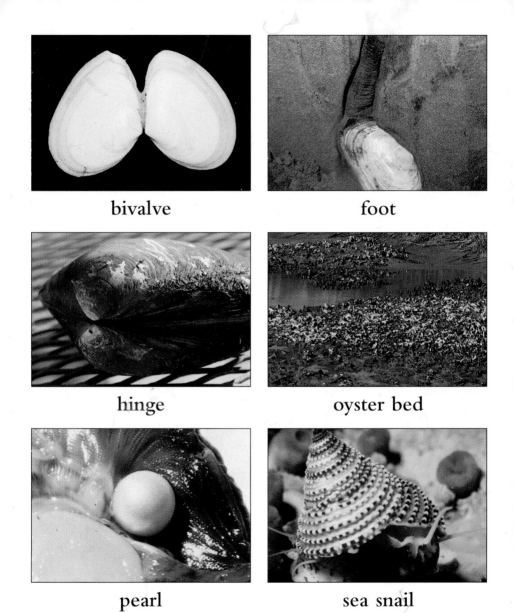

bivalve

foot

hinge

oyster bed

pearl

sea snail

31

Index

bivalve, 10-22, 26, 31

clam, 10, 19, 21

conch, 24, 30

coral reef, 21

crab, 7

cray fish, 7

crustacean, 7, 30

fish, 3, 5, 29

foot, 14-15, 31

giant clam, 21

hinge, 11, 13, 31

insects, 7

lobster, 7

mollusk, 24, 30

mother-of-pearl, 22, 26-27

mussels, 10, 18-19

oyster, 10, 18-19, 23

oyster bed, 18, 31

pearl, 22-23, 26, 31

scallop, 10, 16, 19, 30

sea shore, 29

sea snail, 25, 31

shells, 5, 9-13, 16, 27, 28

shrimp, 7

About the Author

Allan Fowler is a freelance writer with a background in advertising. Born in New York, he lives in Chicago now and enjoys traveling.

Photo Credits

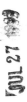